PLAYREADERS

Little sister

Kaye Umansky

MACMILLAN EDUCATION

THE CAST

Chief Strong Ox

Running Deer

Flying Hawk

Darting Fish

Little Sister

The Voices
of the Wind

The Bear

The Deer

The Otter

The White Eagle

First published 1986
Reprinted 1987

Published by
MACMILLAN EDUCATION LTD
Houndmills, Basingstoke,
Hampshire RG21 2XS
and London
Companies and representatives
throughout the world

Typeset by
Regent Typesetting, Odiham

Illustrated by David Dowland and
Joyce Smith

Printed in Hong Kong

British Library Cataloguing
in Publication Data
Umansky, Kaye
Little sister. — (Playreaders)
I. Title II. Series
428.6   PE1119
ISBN 0-333-39380-5

(The wigwam of Chief Strong Ox with Chief in it.
Enter Running Deer, Flying Hawk, Darting Fish and
Little Sister.)

Chief:

Come in my sons. I wish to speak to you.

Darting Fish:

Go away Little Sister. Father wanted to see
the boys.

Little Sister:

I can stay, can't I Daddy?

3

Chief:

Yes if you keep very quiet. Now my sons. You are growing tall. It is time you stopped playing games and became true Indian braves.

Flying Hawk:

At last. What must we do, Father?

Chief:

Each of you must go and look for a white eagle's feather. When you find one and wear it in your hair you will become an Indian brave.

Running Deer:

When can we leave? Tomorrow?

Chief:

Go when you are ready. Keep your arrows sharp and may the spirits guide you.

Little Sister:

Daddy?

Chief:

What, little daughter?

Little Sister:
I want a white eagle's feather too.

Running Deer:
You?

Flying Hawk:
You're a girl.

Darting Fish:
Squaws don't wear white eagle's feathers.

Little Sister:
Why not? My arrows fly as straight as yours.

Chief:
True, daughter. But your job is to cook the meals and dance. Hunting is for braves.

Little Sister:
I don't want to hunt. But I do want an eagle's feather.

Chief:
Run and play, daughter. Good luck, my sons.

(Outside the wigwam.)

Running Deer:

I am Running Deer. I shall run west across the plains to look for the white eagle.

Flying Hawk:

I am Flying Hawk. I shall fly north up to the mountains.

Darting Fish:

I am Darting Fish. I shall swim south down the river. Goodbye Little Sister.

(The brothers leave.)

Little Sister:

They have gone without me. Why can't I have a white eagle's feather? It's not fair.

(The Wind blows in.)

Little Sister:

Who's there? Oh, it's only the Wind.

Wind:

What's the matter, Little Sister?

Little Sister:

I want a white eagle's feather too.

Wind:

Then come with me. I can help you.

Little Sister:

Hooray. I've got my bow and arrows. I'm ready. Which way?

Wind:

To the forest, Little Sister, to the forest.

Little Sister:

Lead on Wind. I'll follow you. And I shan't come back until I've got a white eagle's feather.

(Exit Little Sister and the Wind.)

(Enter Little Sister and the Wind.)

Little Sister:

Well I suppose this is the forest. But I can't see a white eagle.

(Enter Bear.)

Little Sister:

Stand still, Bear. My arrow's pointing at you.

Bear:

Hallo Little Sister. Where are you going?

Little Sister:

To find a white eagle's feather. The Wind's helping me. But first I must kill you.

Bear:

Why? I shan't hurt you. You can share my honey. Here – try some.

Little Sister:

Oh, it does taste sweet. Thank you Bear. I shan't kill you now. Where next, Wind?

Wind:

To the plains, Little Sister, to the plains.

Bear:

I'll give you a ride Little Sister.

SCENE 3

(Enter Little Sister, Bear and Wind.)

Little Sister:

Thank you for the lift Bear. Goodbye.

Bear:

Goodbye Little Sister. Good luck.

(The Bear leaves.)

Little Sister:

Well Wind, here we are on the plains. I can't see a white eagle.

Wind:

Sssshhhhhh.

(Enter Deer.)

Deer:

Oh. You frightened me. Hallo, Little Sister.

Little Sister:

Don't move. I'm going to kill you with my bow and arrow.

Deer:

How will my babies live without a mother? Put down your bow and try some of these sweet red berries.

Little Sister:

Oh, thank you. I love red berries.

(She eats them.)

Deer:

Where are you going, Little Sister?

Little Sister:

To find a white eagle's feather. The Wind is helping me. Where next, Wind?

Wind:

To the river, Little Sister, to the river.

Deer:

I'm going that way. Get on my back. I'll give you a ride.

(Little Sister climbs on. They all leave.)

SCENE 4

(Enter Little Sister, Deer and Wind.)

Little Sister:

Thank you for the ride Deer. Goodbye.

Deer:

Goodbye Little Sister. Good luck.

(The Deer leaves.)

Little Sister:

Well, here's the river. It looks very deep.
There's an island in the middle. What do we
do now?

Wind:

Sssshhhhhh.

(Enter Otter.)

Little Sister:

Stay still, Otter. My arrow is pointing at you.

Otter:

Hallo, Little Sister. Where are you going?

Little Sister:

To find a white eagle's feather. The Wind is helping me. But first, I'm going to kill you.

Otter:

I was going to have some fish for my dinner. Would you like one?

Little Sister:

Why, that's kind of you.

Otter:

Make a fire, then. I know you like your fish to be cooked. So you're looking for the White Eagle?

Little Sister:

Yes. Where do we go next, Wind?

Wind:

To the island, Little Sister, to the island.

Little Sister:

The island? But I can't swim that far.

Otter:

But I can. You can ride on my back. You won't even get your feet wet. But first, let's have our dinner.

(Cook fish and sit round the fire eating it.)

(The island. The Eagle is preening his feathers on top of a tall rock. A canoe is tethered on the other side of the island. Enter Otter, Little Sister and Wind.)

Little Sister:

Thank you for the ride. You were right. I'm not at all wet.

Otter:

Goodbye Little Sister, good luck.

(Otter swims off.)

Little Sister:

Well here is the rocky island but where is the Eagle? What do we do Wind?

Wind:
Climb the rock, Little Sister, climb the rock.

Little Sister:
Right, here goes. It looks very high. I hope I don't fall.

(She climbs the rock.)

18

SCENE 6

(The top of the rock. The White Eagle is preening its feathers. Enter Little Sister and Wind.)

Little Sister:

At last. The White Eagle. Look, Wind, it's the White Eagle.

Wind:

Sssssshhhhh.

Eagle:

Aaarrkk. And who are you?

19

Little Sister:

I'm Little Sister. I've come to shoot you. I want one of your white feathers to wear in my hair.

Eagle:

Ah but if you shoot me, my feathers will become red. I thought you wanted a white feather.

Little Sister:

I do. Oh dear. What shall I do?

Eagle:

How many animals did you shoot on the way here?

Little Sister:

Why – none. They all helped me, you see. They were kind, and gave me food and carried me on their backs.

Eagle:

Then your bow and arrows didn't help you get what you want, did they?

Little Sister:

Well – no.

Eagle:

If you have learnt that, you have become wise. My feathers may only be worn by those who are both brave and wise.

Little Sister:

Then can I have one?

Eagle:

Help yourself from my tail. But put down your bow and arrows first.

(Little Sister does so. She takes a feather and puts it in her hair.)

Little Sister:

Thank you Eagle. I shall wear it all the time.

Eagle:

Are you going home now?

Little Sister:

Soon. But first I want to see what is round the bend in the river.

Eagle:

Look down. What do you see floating on the water far below?

Little Sister:

Why, it's a little canoe.

Eagle:

Climb on my back. We'll fly down together.

(They go down.)

SCENE 7

(*The canoe. Enter Little Sister, Eagle and Wind.*)

Little Sister:

Thank you for everything, Eagle.

Eagle:

Little Sister, you've left your bow and arrows on the rock.

Little Sister:

Never mind, I don't need them now.

23

Eagle:

Then goodbye. Safe journey.

Little Sister:

Goodbye Eagle.

(Eagle flies off, Little Sister climbs into the canoe.)

Little Sister:

Oh there's no paddle. Will you blow me, Wind

Wind:

I will, Little Sister, I will.

Little Sister:

I wonder if my brothers got their feathers. I'll know when I get home. But where are we going first, Wind?

Wind:

Whooo knows, Little Sister, whooooo knows?